THE
AWESTRUCK
AND THE
MOONSTRUCK

THE
AWESTRUCK
AND THE
MOONSTRUCK

J. DUCHAK

For more information, email:
jduchakpoetry@yahoo.com

J. Duchak
Instagram: @jduchakpoetry
Facebook: JDuchak Poetry

First Paperback/Hardcover Edition March 2024

ISBN:
979-8-9894652-0-0 (Paperback)
979-8-9894652-1-7 (Hardcover)
979-8-9894652-2-4 (eBook)

Library of Congress Control Number: 2023924259

Edited by Shelby Leigh (1st edit), J. Duchak (final edits).
Cover design by Islam Farid.
Interior design by Karolina Wudniak, karolinawudniak.com.
Blurb by Book Blurb Magic, IG: @bookblurbmagic.
Illustrations by J. Duchak (Using GoArt PRO AI image generator for iOS) Islam Farid (cover), Karolina Wudniak (dedication page).

…dedicated to she and her—
two sides of the same coin,
two heads from the one
heart of inspiration,
who left me with poetic tales to pen,
whenever I answered her call.

–J. Duchak, 2023

Contents

A Self-Inked Odyssey

Art in life, I create
In communion with the unseen.
Helpers, loved ones, and guides
Steer my heart in certain directions,
Allowing me to craft my craft,
Metamorphosing my voice
Into wings of an eagle,
Or those of the butterfly,
Making hearts flutter
While I soar
Beyond the beliefs of
What is possible.

I rewrite the story
Others tried to pen for me,
To ground my continuous flight
Onwards to the light.
My eyes face the storm
I had shied away from yesterday.
Clouds part and sunrays
Light my way
When I proceed
With a fearless faith facing
Tomorrow, with a stoicism
Only matched by grand warriors
In the battle of life.

I no longer have a battle to fight.
The war may rage on,
But I fly beyond it,
As there is no war
If both no longer play the game.
My sword is in its scabbard,
Put down, though ready to slay.
Obstacles may arise,
But when I hold love in my heart,
The roadblocks disappear.

The destination forged
Was not an endpoint,
But a mere layover.
Ten minutes or ten years,
I may rest, though I hold
Steady in my heart
The vision of you,
Lingering in my mind.

When I first took flight,
You were my compass,
But also my destiny.
My reason to move
Through the freezing winds,
And a shield to
Block the sun at midday,
So my wings don't burn.
I fly as high as the sun,
An ongoing odyssey
Venturing towards you,
The legend I have lived for,
Denounced by others as mere myth,
But I know you are out there,
And I will find you.

In the heat of summer
Or in a cave, stranded in the Arctic,
When I finally find you,
I will have transformed into
A version of myself capable of
Loving you and allowing me
To accept your love.
Even if the time comes to depart again,
When you are with me
I will always be home.

If I Run to Catch Her

If I run to catch her,
She will simply fly away.
She flutters her wings softly,
When I gaze into her eyes.
As she stands still,
My mind stops turning and
She is at peace with me.

I wish to hold her in my hand.
For that, I have to catch her.
As I quickly reach, she flies away,
Around and around, giving me
A chance to stop, but I keep running.
Dripping with sweat and out of breath,
I can't help but come to a pause.
She is out of sight, long gone.
A butterfly, meant to soar
And simply remind others
Of the beauty life holds,
If they can wake up from
The sleep of their comfy cocoon.

As her memory leaves my mind,
I digress and decide to go home.
In that moment there she is,
On the tip of my nose,
Slowly flapping her wings,
Gazing again into my eyes.
She is love, telling me to stop running,
As it will continue to elude me,
But if I stop and let it catch me,
Love is mine forever.

The Right Time?

There's no time,
Like the right time,
An opportune time
To seize an opportunity,
Or open our arms to love,
Though when is the right time?

Is there ever a right time?
Life's magic is in the fleeting
Moments of spontaneity and awe,
When we least expect it.
When we are looking
For a shooting star,
Its presence eludes us.

When we say we are ready,
We wait for opportunities
That never seem to appear.
But in the times we live life,
Without expectations or hoping
For the outcome to be our way,
We are ever surprised by
Wonders we never dreamed of—
Lovers who find us in
The winter of life and
Carry us home, so
They can sing with us in Springtime.
Once in a lifetime chances,
Held not for
The highest bidder, but
For the willing and eager.

It's not about being perfect,
To receive all you have wished for.
Through accepting imperfections
And letting others see them,
Someone special may surprise you,
Magically walking into your life and
Maybe you'll say, "She's perfect".

The Wonder Wishing Well

He walked down
The misty meadows of a
Foggy Friday morning,
To gather water from the well,
After being sweetly awakened
By the sound of a songbird,
Who visits his window every morning.

He travels to the bottom of the hill,
When he sees a woman struggling
With an empty well.
Needing water for himself,
He approaches her, and his heart stops.
He's stunned as he looks
At a mirror staring back,
Her beautiful face, dimmed
By a pensive countenance,
And a near empty pail.

He starts to speak to her
About what's happening in her life.
They ended up sitting beside the
Well, and talking about the hope
They have for tomorrow,
And where they are looking to go.

Destined for change and travel,
He the traveler, never allowing
His roots to penetrate and
Claim the ground he walks on, while
She journeys through her mind.
Dreams float into her thoughts
As if they are reality when awake,
Seeing others more grand
Than how she sees herself.
If only she saw what he sees,
When he looks on in wonder.

He stays with her, comforts her,
And gives her the confidence
To confront the challenges
That lie in front of her,
Instead of simply moving on like him
When things get tough.
He offers his ear, his heart, and
His empathy to be present with her.
As they resign to the idea of
Collecting water for the days ahead
And accept the notion of
Being thirsty for the day,
The misty, ignored sky they sit under
Suddenly turns to thick grey clouds.

A tickle, a drizzle, a downpour,
And an overwhelming deluge of hope
Swarms them, as the well
Catches every drop of summer rain
It can possibly hold.

As they fill each other's bucket,
They look at each other's eyes
In wonder. They smile, nod, and
Start the trek home.
She goes her way, he goes his.
He says to her, "I'll be here tomorrow."
The woman says, "So will I.
I have all I can hold right now,
But your endless well of kindness,
Filled my parched heart today
And I'd like to do the same tomorrow
For you—
Let me tear down the dam
That blocks me from
Getting closer to your heart."

Through the Fields of August Sunflowers

Come run with me,
Through the towering
Sunflower fields of August…
Just you and I.
We'll get lost and hide
For a while,
From each other and
The rest of the world.
We'll sneak up and find each other,
Chase the innocence of youth in
Endless rows, as bees kiss the flowers.

Through all our running,
Maybe life will guide us,
To meet in the middle,
So this bee can kiss
The beautiful flower you are,
Love and leave,
With a promise to return
Each morning.
Whether in the towering sunflower fields,
Or through etheric fields,
We run side by side
Sharing the beauty
Of this world we see.

The Wanderer and the Poet

He was a wanderer and a poet,
A poet and a dreamer, a dreamer
Who dreamt of nothing but love.
Floating through life,
The years went by like a parade.
Always simply an onlooker,
Never riding any of the floats.

He still continued to watch
As the strong winds of life
Tore the calendar sheets off the wall,
Which left him unaffected and stationary.
He continued to write and
Observe all the love in his mind
And feelings in his heart,

Lost in nostalgia and
Could-have-beens
Rather than what could be.
He put his pen down,
Gazed around and took in
All of it, rather than just a snapshot—
His perception of life's landscape.

The parade nears its end,
And the man decides to head home.
He looks down at his
Untied laces and a silver coin,
Adjacent to his right foot.
He laced his boots, gathered the silver,
And looked up.
He saw a stunning young woman,
Smiling down on him,
With a sparkle more blinding
Than his silver coin's reflection,
Flipping in the afternoon sun.
She reached outwards with one hand
As he exclaims, "Finally."
The woman says, "You were
Not ready for this before."
With that, the poet looks
At his book, which spanned
Most of his adult life,
And without a second thought
Threw it out of sight.

He knew standing in front of him,
Was something greater than any words
He could ever conjure up.

She says, "It's nice to have you here finally."
The poet says, "Yes, I thought you may never come."
She asks why he threw out the journal.
He says, "There's no need for it anymore;
What I was writing about is now in front of me.
I no longer need to wish for you,
I would rather just love you instead."
The pair look at each other and smile,
Holding each other's hand,
Looking forward to wherever
The parade route takes them.

May Wedding in Spain

I dreamed in the rain,
I dreamed of a May wedding in Spain,
I always hoped my dreams would come true,
Nothing less would ever seem to do,
Though the greatest dream
Came when I met you.

Perpetual Night

This night with her, I never wish to end.
Let there be perpetual moonlight forever,
As we watch the waves break and
See the starlight shine down upon us.

We frolic in the ocean's tide holding hands;
The strongest waves cannot separate us,
Or bring us to our knees.
We peer out into this glimmering grand sea of infinity,
And I wonder, is she wishing for me, as I am for her?

If this night is a mere illusion,
An ethereal eternity met only in dreams,
Never wake me. If I am awake,
Never let my eyes concede to sleep again,
As no dream can ever compare to her.

After a final sweet embrace,
We say goodnight for what
Seems like the last time.
I watch her walk away—
Her beautiful white flowing gown
Illuminates in the moonlight.

She is my dream, manifest,
Though more magical and magnificent.
I had a vision, but life had the blueprint,
Something better in store.
Awestruck and moonstruck,
I watch with wondrous love
How life can create her
More graceful and beautiful
Than I could possibly ever dream of.

The Elusive

I seek the elusive.
I want the sunrise,
But not the sun,
A shooting star,
But not the moon,
The uncertain,
Not the certain.
In this life…
I want her.

Step Into my Heart

Take my hand,
Like I have taken yours.
I need your strength
To guide me tonight,
Through the darkness.
Scaling the many walls,
Side-stepping pitfalls—
Pain purposely placed
To keep others out.
Take me back with
Your light, a beacon,
A lighthouse, shining bright
In my life's current storm.
The raging waters ahead
I can safely sail,
As long as your light
Comes with me.
Guide the way back home;
You are welcome there,
If you step through
The door to my heart.

The Onlooker's Horizon

We grip each other's hands and hold each other close.
Walking down winding pathways,
The road leads us to an impasse.
We decide we must walk
On our own for a bit.
Certain lengths, we must walk alone,
In order to grow closer together.
When we catch up on the other side,
We come together again,
Meeting at the onlooker's horizon.

In years past I have visited
This wooden deck overlooking the river,
Rotted and beaten it had become,
It has since been fully restored,
Its foundation solid once again.

She and I connect, as we
Watch the slow surf run upstream,
Talking about dreams
For the future and past lovers.
Her presence helps heal
The damage of an ill-hearted woman's wrath,

That etched a target for others
To do the same,
Erased by the grace of her fingertips,
The warmth of her smile,
And the glow of her eyes,
Which light the way to eternity.

As the clouds pour in,
So do boisterous visitors
Whose presence cannot
Stop the music of two
Who love and value each other.

We see the dark and shine
Blinding light on old wounds,
To hold and heal each other,
Becoming whole again,
For another to complement,
Not complete them.

A pair like this is rare,
The prototype for an
Alchemical marriage of
Those who strive for
The highest ground—
A journey through
The ethers and layers
Beyond the sun,
To come out
The other side as one.

A Robin's Song

Sunny morning blue skies hang high
While the covering of the chateau
Keeps her sleeping in the shadows,
Till it's time for her eyes to rise and greet the day.

Outside her room, is an open terrace
With two archways, supported by two Roman pillars.
Pink and blue hydrangeas congregate
In bushes which line the ledge outside.

An American Robin has made his home
Inside the bushes.
Every morning he waits,
Long past his wake time,
To be greeted
By her lovely voice.
He could flock with the others,
Competing with calls creating
A chorus of cacophony,
In the early morning hours.
Instead, he stays silent
And waits for her.

When he hears her voice,
Her call to him every morning,
He moves his head to
Bask in her beauty.
Slowly he begins
Singing his sincere song
Meant for her, though
Others are welcome to listen.
His attention to her is unwavering,
And his loyalty unbridled.
For a time each morning,
They get to share a moment.

He chooses the hydrangea bushes
Outside her room to nest
Because he loves the vibrant
Blue beauties of those bushes.
He never saw anything
As beautiful as her on a
Monday May morning,
So he makes it a point to
Wait for her to wake each day
As her beauty is
The inspiration for him to sing again.
His tune, once meant for another,
Is solely dedicated to her now.

When she goes to bed each night,
He speaks to her
In wishful whispers, saying, "Goodnight.
All great things I wish for you… always,
My Love."

Safety Found in Safe Hearts

I want you to know
You are safe in my
Presence and in my arms.
Never will I sneak a kiss,
That is undeserved,
Or take your hand in dance,
Without you spelling it out,
With your actions or words…
I'll let you complete that sentence.

Bringing a Lonely Lover to Light

Drifting along at sea,
In rhythm with the undulating ocean waves,
Inundated by the sound of slow wave breaks,
I hear a voice in the distance.
Without any food for a few,
I wonder… Is this real,
Or just the substance of dreams?

I sail along, and the voice gets louder,
From afar, I see her—
A young maiden in the distance,
Singing on the cliffside.
Just like the watchmen or the lighthouse keeper,
This is her post,
To draw lonely seafarers to land.

Wary of stories of sultry, singing sirens,
I proceed with curiosity and a hint of caution.
I knew I was close to land,
But didn't expect such a harmonious welcome.

As I dock, I lift my head and
She looks right into my eyes,
Eyes so beautiful they would shatter emeralds.

As the maiden still sings,
I feel I am floating.
My journey has ended and
Life's maelstroms have subsided, for now.

I climb the steps to the cliffside to meet her.
My weary eyes can see a golden pink aura around her.
She stands proud and tall,
With a gown gorgeously glowing in the afternoon sun.
Her long curly brown locks
Blow in the wind, covering her face,
But cannot quell her voice.

She sings her song,
Whether there is an audience
Of none, ten, or a hundred
She knows the unseen onlookers
Hear every note she sings,
As she sends gratitude
For the gift bestowed upon her.

I finally reach the top of the cliffside,
Where she stands, still singing.
She looks at me and
Gives a glowing smile.
With a penetrating gaze of light,
She reaches out with both hands,
As if to save me from my savage past.

I take her hands and am
Embraced by her light,
The invisible shackles come undone,
The mental prison gates finally open,
And the ramparts of my heart crumble;
I can now walk forward with her.

We walk down a luminous path
Towards a door of blinding light.
When we arrive at the doorway,
She stops and gives a nod,
Blowing a soft kiss to say goodbye,
To signify she can bring me
Back to the light, but I am the only one
Who can step back into it.

Stay and Sway, or Fly Away?

Come, sway in place
Or leave for the day.
Leaning on the gate
At the marina, I watch the river
Fill with traffic in the summer heat,
Sweat stings my eyes,
And her departure onwards,
Stabs my heart and punches my gut.

I the wanderer; she the traveler
Always moving across the map.
So she goes, while I travel in my mind,
And so it is but a dream
She would stay for the summer—
A promise unkept, when the allure
Of life's gold lies in California.
The itch of August,
With its lonely winds,
Wants us to drift forward.
Sailing in different directions,
She runs with the wind,
But always misses her destination.

I go my own way,
With my boat still docked in port.
All I had to do was wake up
From the summer morning dream,
And I saw she was just a bird,
Riding the sky, never grounded,
Here for a moment,
Just to say goodbye.

My December Winter

My mind knows the answer,
But my heart does not want to accept it.
When I said I loved you,
And waited for a response
But never got one,
The unspoken language of rejection
Stabbed me, but also set me free.

Freedom, born on this fourth of July,
An ironic day of independence
For this country I dwell,
But for me as well.
Freedom from an idea
Of a future with you,
That will never come true.
You, a rare songbird,
Free in the night,
Stopped by my window for a moment.
As hard as I tried,
I could never catch you,
Let alone cage you.

My heart still cries songs
To call you back,
But they all fall flat,
As your absence is sharp,
A shard that cut me.
As painful as it is,
It reminded me I can still feel
Love for another and anguish
When that love is gone.
You are free
And may fly away.
Do not call out to me,
If you do not wish to stay
And plant seeds for a Summertime love.
If you choose to
Fly south and let me fall,
When you depart
For the warmth of another,
Then I will certainly freeze
In a late December Winter.

17

Love Nocturnal

When we said goodbye,
I thought I was at peace;
Well, I lied. When we first met
I held an objective look,
A hope for a future with you,
With a slight sense of resignation,
If we never met again.

Was this goodbye forever?
I don't know, but as
The last minutes with you
Vanished in a mere blink,
Ending with your nervous wink,
I never wanted to let you go.

After a final embrace,
Love eternal met impermanence.
As fleeting visions of you
Started to fly away,
I tried to hold onto the visions,
Though I saw it was futile.
My love to live
In a waking dream,
Was merely the substance
Of love nocturnal.

Wind Gusts Of Youth

In the midnight wind,
I felt the essence of my youth,
A firestorm of overwhelming emotion
Both of singing sweetness and longing,
Loves lost, gone, or never were.

I hear the music play
As the wheel turns.
I slip into a veritable vortex,
Which takes me back to
The decade of my early youth.
This was a time when all seemed possible,
Limitless was the palette
Dreams were painted with,
A longing for a simmering love.

No common superficial love would do.
Only the ultimate sought—the elusive soulmate
Torn apart from each other
At soul's inception,
Running, crying, and hoping,
To reconnect through lives past.

I bask in the time of my youth—
A time of pseudo-Victorian era hopeful romanticism.
A sentiment so pervasive to the fabric of my life,
It allowed me to dream for the future,
Even if reality was buried in sand,
And invisible fires were started
That later burned our current era
Into a lifeless, barren field.

I slip in and out,
As the time is fleeting,
And the images fade.
A temporary respite reminds me
I can still dream,
Even if some of the colors
I painted with,
Have run with time.

He, the Treasure She Looks for

One day, she'll be looking
For someone like me,
Maybe in the spaces between
Night and dawn, day and dusk,
In cold rainy moments, in her Fall.
The memories will flood her mind
Of someone who looked on in awe,
But was equally content,
Just to share a conversation.

I let her go, so I can be free.
I let the nomad roam.
Maybe she'll realize
What she is looking for
Is right where she stands.
She doesn't have to fly to the moon,
To find what treasures
Tomorrow's tide may bring in.

Summer Night Interlude

I couldn't accompany you
To the party this evening,
Though I bet you looked stunning
Amongst all the lights at night,
Strung in rows across and around the gazebo,
Where we would sit alone.
In the shadows of all others dancing,
We look on, content
Just to be next to each other.

The music is still playing,
As the night is steadily aging,
The crowd noise is getting softer,
But the night and the band play on.
The moonlight is reflected
Ever so brightly in your eyes,
But your smile
Is what relaxes my head to
The side, as I lean forward to
Kiss you for the very first time.
Lips unlock and I see through time;
This is not the first time
I've kissed you.

We Don't Know...Yet

Come with me today
To watch the sunrise,
Before summer ends.
Are you leaving at the end?
We both don't know yet.
Will the clouds break,
Just in time, so we see the sun
Say, "Good Morning," as it
Peers and rears its head
Over the horizon?
We don't know yet.

Like the sunrise
You are fleeting,
And just like the rising sun
Runs to meet the sky,
I scramble to catch you.
If I can catch you,
You are mine,
But if I am too slow,
Rise like the magnificent beauty
You are to become,
Above the pettiness

Of a terrestrial landscape,
High above for all
To see the luminescence
Your essence radiates.

It would be the best,
If you turned out to be mine,
Though I now realize,
No matter if you leave or stay,
I will somehow, someway,
See you shine.
Whether it is one more day,
Or at the end of my days,
I will see you rise again.

I would rather
See you happy,
Than see you be mine,
If that is what your heart
And fate decide, but then again,
We don't know yet...